Kindle Fire HD Apps: The Top 50 Kindle Apps for the HD

Discover the 50 Best Apps for your Kindle Fire HD!

By Francis Monico

Table of Contents

Introduction to the Amazon Appstore 4

Business Apps 5

    Evernote 6

    LinkedIn 7

    Wi-Fi File Explorer Pro 8

    YCard – Youlu Card Reader 9

    Cisco WebEx Meetings 10

Finance Apps 11

    Mint.com Personal Finance 12

    Bloomberg Kindle Tablet Edition 13

    Debt Payoff Planner 14

    EasyMoney 15

    MyTaxRefund by Turbo Tax 16

Children's Apps 17

    The Cat in the Hat 18

    Kids Ultimate Finger Painting 19

    VeggieTales: The League of Incredible Vegetables 20

    Minecraft Pocket Edition 21

    Sight Words Sentence Builder 22

Productivity apps 23

    Office Suite Professional 6 24

    iTranslate 25

    Dropbox 26

    Speaktoit Assistant 27

    ezPDF Reader 28

Lifestyles and Utilities Apps 29

    Virtual Makeover 30

    Prayers & Blessings Daily 31

    textPlus Free 32

    7notes Premium – Smart Writing Tool 33

    SAS Survival Guide 34

Health and Fitness Apps 35

Rain Therapy: Rest, Relax, Unwind 36

Calorie Counter and Diet Tracker by MyFitnessPal 37

All-in Yoga (Kindle Tablet Edition) 38

WebMD (Kindle Tablet Edition) 39

Home Remedies (Free) 40

Sports Apps 41

NBA Game Time (Kindle tablet edition) 42

ESPN ScoreCenter 43

Yahoo! Fantasy Football '12 44

College Football Scoreboard 45

MLB.com At Bat Lite 46

Entertainment Apps 47

Netflix 48

Hulu Plus (Kindle Tablet Edition) 49

Ghost Radar: LEGACY 50

Eye Illusions Free 2.3 51

Scanner Radio Pro 52

Game Apps 53

Cut the Rope 54

Andoku Sudoku 2 Free 55

Angry Birds Space HD (Kindle Tablet Edition) 56

Asphalt 7: Heat (Kindle Tablet Edition) 57

Pac-Man 58

News & Magazines Apps 59

Wall Street Journal (Fire App/WSJ Digital) 60

NBC Nightly News 61

TIME Magazine 62

National Geographic Magazine 63

PEOPLE Magazine 64

Introduction to the Amazon App Store

Welcome to the amazing App Store for Android by Amazon.com! Here you will find a wide variety of apps for all purposes. From Business Apps to Children's Apps, anything you are looking for is just a search away.

In this e-book, we will look at a variety of apps from 10 different categories. These are some of the best apps on the market in their respective category. We have chosen the following 50 apps because they are the most helpful, the best designed, the most popular, and the most fun!

By utilizing these 50 apps you will be able to increase your productivity, gain access to necessary business functions on-the-go, and take a well-deserved break when time allows. Read on to find out more about the Top 50 apps for Kindle Fire HD.

Business Apps

In this section, we look at the 5 most useful business apps. These apps will be helpful for mostly business purposes, although they may prove helpful in other areas of your life. We've chosen the following 5 apps based on how beneficial they are in either conducting business, helping procure new business, or a combination of the two.

These apps are ideal for any busy businessman or women looking to streamline their business life. By utilizing these all-encompassing applications you can reduce a cluttered workspace and maximize your working time.

Evernote

Price: $0.00 (Premium Service is available $45 for the year, or $5 per month)
Purpose: Capture and save any ideas, notes, images, websites, or anything else possible that you come across in one easy to access location across any of your devices.

Key Benefits:
- Keep everything in sync – Use Evernote across all of your devices because everything will be synced.
- Research Organization – Gathering information for a new client proposal has never been easier. Anything you highlight, find, take a snapshot of, can all be in one place.
- Easy Business Travel – You can keep all of your travel itineraries, reservations, bookings, directions, and travel tips all in one location within Evernote.
- Record Anything – You can record any web address, image, audio clip, video clip and save it to one location.

Overview:
This app, across all devices and app stores, is considered one of the most useful business and productivity suites of the last decade. Note taking and archiving have never been simpler, and the amount of data storage you receive for the free version is plenty. Save all of your data, notes, images, recordings, and more into your "notebooks" and use the simple search function to recall this data instantly.

Every businessperson should find this app instantly useful. For those with extensive storage needs, looking to take their work offline, or work collaboratively with others on their notes, should consider the premium option.

LinkedIn

Price: $0.00 (Premium – Business Account available at $239.40 per year paid in advance, Business Plus Account available at $479.40 per year paid in advance or $49.95 per month if paid monthly, or Executive Account available at $899.40 per year in advance)
Purpose: Do everything that you can do on your LinkedIn account normally, just from your Kindle Fire HD!

Key Benefits:
- Full access to profiles – You can easily view every public profile within the LinkedIn network.
- Make new connections – Everyone you meet can now be your newest connection right when you meet them.
- Respond to messages – View and reply to all your personal messages on the go.
- Manage your network – Respond to network invitations on the go.
- Search the entire LinkedIn network anywhere, anytime

Overview:
When you need to be connected, you must have this app! The ability to access your network at any time no matter where you are is a freedom that is necessary for any busy professional. The app provides complete access to all of the important account features based on your current account level. Upgrades to account available via purchase of Premium Accounts as stated above. With the LinkedIn App, you have complete access to your account just as you would from your pc on any mobile device with at least Android 2.1.

Networking has always been considered an invaluable business tool. If you want customers, you have to get yourself and your product or service out there. Now you have the ability to share updates, reply to messages, and join new networks on the spot! No more waiting until you are back at the office or at home and trying to remember the name of the important business contact you just met.

Wi-Fi File Explorer Pro

Price: $0.99
Purpose: Gives you the ability to transfer files from your PC or Laptop to your Kindle Fire or other Android device in seconds without a connector cable.

Key Benefits:
- Easy file transfer – Allows you to easily manage files between your PC/Laptop and Android devices.
- Security when and where you need it – Secure Wi-Fi connection keeps your files safe as you view and transfer them.
- Added security features – Safe password-protected Web browser.
- Streaming – Stream music directly to your PC from your Android device.
- Personalized settings – User-controlled port configurations for added control.

Overview:
Wi-Fi File Explorer Pro gives you the useful ability to transfer virtually any file from your PC/Laptop to your Android device. Whether you need to access a presentation quickly to share with potential investors or customers, or you just want to hear your favorite song on the way to work, this App makes it easier than ever! No longer will you have to lug around a USB cable everywhere you go.

The Pro version gives you many additional features over the free version, including the ability to upload, sync, delete, copy, zip and unzip every file on your Android or computer. Simply connect both devices to the Wi-Fi Network, access the Web address, and you have all of your files at your fingertips!

YCard – Youlu Card Reader

Price: $0.00
Purpose: Scan business cards to add new contacts easily and accurately.

Key Benefits:
- Accurate scanning – No longer will you have to fumble around with business cards and worry about losing important contacts.
- Contact sharing – Want to send some contact information to a friend? It's quick and easy now to exchange already scanned cards.
- Group/Search – Keep your contacts together by grouping them into relevant categories and search to find them quickly when you need them.
- Real-time backup – Never lose another contact. Once your image is scanned it is immediately backed up.

Overview:
YCard gives you an easy solutions to keeping a rolodex of business cards and contacts. Now within seconds you can scan, group, and backup every business contact you get. You can do this anytime anywhere. Never worry about missing out on a business opportunity again! Each time someone hands you a business card you can quickly scan the card into YCard. Your scan will be read accurately to add the contact information to the appropriate place. Choose groups for your contacts based on various terms. Quickly find your contacts when you need them using the search feature.

Need to share your contacts? No problem! You can easily exchange business card images right from your Android device. Each scan is backed up in real time so you never have to worry about losing a connection again, and you save space in your purse or briefcase by getting rid of all those paper cards. Take your Kindle Fire HD or other Android device to conferences or anywhere you may acquire new business contacts and look professional and organized! Support is offered for many popular languages including English, Simplified Chinese, Traditional Chinese, Korean, and Japanese.

Cisco WebEx Meetings

Price: $0.00

Purpose: High-quality 2-way video conferencing with voice so you can attend meetings no matter where you are from your Kindle Fire HD or other Android device.

Key Benefits:

- High-quality video feed – See all the details you need to in incredible HD quality.
- Voice controls – Voice activated features such as video switching allow you to quickly switch to see the next person who is talking with just a few words rather than your hands.
- Host or join meetings – You can host your own meeting and invite others to it or join any meeting from the email invite you received.
- Detailed meeting information – Once in a meeting you will see the attendee list, take a closer look at any shared content, go into a private chat or group chat within the meeting, and zoom and scan to get a better look at what your colleagues are trying to show you.

Overview:

With Cisco Systems WebEx Meetings, you will never be late for a web conference again. Join no matter where you are right from your Kindle Fire HD or other Android enabled device. Meetings are free to attend for anyone. You can join from My Meeting List, the link in an email invite, by the meeting number, or the Cisco Homepage.

Various feature let you have total control over your conference experience. Meetings are available in 13 languages. Within meetings you have the option to go into private or group chats making group activities a breeze. View the full attendee list or take your conference into full-screen so you won't be distracted. This is a must-have app for any professional that takes their work seriously.

Finance Apps

In this section, we look at the 5 most useful finance apps. These apps will be helpful for mostly finance purposes, although they may prove helpful in other areas of your life. We've chosen the following 5 apps based on how beneficial they are in helping you organize and control your finances, stay informed on things that will affect your finances, or all of these things.

These apps are ideal for any busy person interested in controlling their finances quickly and easily on the go. By utilizing these applications you can track, monitor, and control your finances with never-before-seen speed and ease.

Mint.com Personal Finance

Price: $0.00 (Requires an account with Mint.com, free registration.)
Purpose: Easily view and track your finances from banks, credit cards, and other financial accounts from your Kindle Fire HD.

Key Benefits:
- See all your information in one place – Mint automatically puts information from all your accounts together.
- Automatic categorization of transactions – Mint automatically separates your transactions by category for you so you save time and stay organized.
- No more late fees – Get email or text alerts for everything from due dates to fees, budgets and low balances.
- Gauranteed security – No worries if you lose or misplace your Android device as you can deactivate access to your account right from your PC.

Overview:
Mint.com is one of the most used financial apps today. It is so popular because it does so much to make tracking your finances simple. Once you create your account, Mint will pull all your account information automatically into one place and separate individual transactions for you.

Create budgets from your actual spending records and modify it anyway you want. Get email or text updates to help you keep track of your budgets, fees, due dates and more. Great features let you do amazing things, like the App Widget Access which lets you see your balance and outstanding debt right on your home screen so you always know how much money you have!

Bloomberg Kindle Tablet Edition

Price: $0.00
Purpose: Bloomberg's financial data service on the go!

Key Benefits:
- Stay on top of Financial data – Bloomberg's editors hand pick the most important financial news stories to help you make smart investment decisions.
- Get the latest information – Everything available from Bloomberg is right at your fingertips like the latest in major equity and currency markets.
- Check your stocks anytime – Create a customized list of stocks then check them where ever you are tracking price changes and the value of your portfolio.

Overview:
Bloomberg has been a trusted name in finance for generations. Now you have the power of information at your fingertips. No matter where you are, there is always time to check in on your favorite stocks or see what's moving the market.

You can create a list of specific stocks or search through them all to find the specific information you are looking for. Check your portfolio position based on the most up-to-date information available on your stocks. You even have access to the latest information on bond and currency markets. Make smart decisions anytime with the Bloomberg app, optimized for Kindle Fire.

Debt Payoff Planner

Price: $0.99

Purpose: Customize a plan to pay off your debt and stick to it in an easy and efficient way.

Key Benefits:

- Easy to use interface – Easy controls make it simple for you to follow the prompts to set up your personal payoff plan.
- Two modes for your skill level – Simple and Advanced Mode to fit your skill level and the level of detail you want to use in creating your plan.
- Export to email – Take charge of your plan by exporting your data to email then printing it so you can go over everything in detail to check for mistakes.

Overview:

Debt is something nearly all Americans have to deal with. Whether it is credit cards or student loans or even medical bills, most likely you have some things you need to get paid off to get your credit under control. Debt Payoff Planner makes it easy to take charge of your debt payoff.

With easy to follow on-screen instructions, adjustable options, and a lot of detail, Debt Payoff Planner allows you to enter all your debt and make a plan to pay it off that you can stick to. You can easily see how long it will take to pay off various debts, change the interest rate if the terms of your debt change, and get an organized layout of your debt so you can decide what is the most important to take care of first.

EasyMoney

Price: $9.95
Purpose: Makes it easy for you to manage your money; control your budget, expenses, and get bill reminders.

Key Benefits:
- Take photos of receipts – Now it is easier than ever to input your expense by taking pictures of your receipts and bills directly from your Kindle Fire HD or other Android device.
- Get payment reminders – Set up notifications for one-time payments and recurring bills.
- Color-coded bar charts – Easily see where your money is going with easy-to-read charts showing monthly expenses by category or by specific account.

Overview:
With 204 5-star reviews, EasyMoney is one of the best rated finance apps on Amazon. Easily keep track of your spending, budget, expenses, and bills by setting up reminders and checking your accounts often. You can get detailed expense reports to help keep yourself on track. Color-coded bar charts show you exactly where your money is going so you can decide where you need to cut back.

MyTaxRefund by Turbo Tax

Price: $0.00
Purpose: This app allows you to check the status of your Income Tax Refund.

Key Benefits:
- Check the status of your return anytime – If you have e-Filed your tax return, you can use this app to check the status.
- Get updates at each stage – No more waiting in the dark. Using this app you can check anytime to if your return has been accepted, what the current status is, and when you will receive your return.

Overview:
MyTaxRefund by Turbo Tax is the must-have app for anyone who e-Files their Federal Income Tax Return. After answering a few quick questions to establish your identity, you will be in the system where you can find out what you need to know about your return.

Quickly see if your return has been accepted or rejected. Check back as often as you like to see any updates on the status of your return. If you are a TurboTax customer, you can get the status of your State Tax Return as well. TurboTax is a trusted company in tax return and filing software so you know your information is safe and secure.

Children's Apps

In this section, we look at the 5 most useful apps for children. These apps will be appealing to children for various reasons. Some may be educational, but all are guaranteed to be fun! We've chosen the following 5 apps based on their appeal to children, their educational value, their fun value, and how easy they are for children to use.

These apps are ideal for those of you with children that wish to entertain or educate your children with apps on your Kindle Fire HD or other Android device. By utilizing these applications for children you can provide your children hours of fun and education to keep them happy, occupied, and learning.

The Cat in the Hat

Price: $3.99
Purpose: This app provides an interactive experience with the classic book "The Cat in the Hat" by Dr. Seuss.

Key Benefits:
- Read how you want – Kids can choose from 3 reading modes – Read to Me, Read it Myself, or Auto Play.
- Professional narration – The Read to Me option is performed by a celebrity speaker in a professional way.
- Music/Sound Effects – The classic story has been reimagined with new sounds and great music.
- Easily read and follow along – Words are highlighted to make it easy for children to follow along or read themselves and words can be touched to repeat them.
- Pop-ups – Images on-screen can be touched and the words will pop up!

Overview:
One of the greatest stories from our childhood has been re-imagined for the technology age that our children are now a part of! Enjoy this classic with your child, and let them experience the wonderful world of Dr. Seuss.

The Cat in the Hat app allows children to choose from 3 reading modes. It also incorporates the touchscreen by allowing images to be touched to get the word to pop up. In addition, a word can be touched to have it repeated in case the child missed it the first time. Colorful classic images combine with new sounds and music to enhance your child's learning experience and capture their attention in a new way!

Kids Ultimate Finger Painting

Price: $0.00

Purpose: Fun drawing app which allows kids to finger paint in different modes for long-term enjoyment.

Key Benefits:

- Full-featured – A drawing app that is filled with options for children to have hours of fun like a built-in puzzle, option to load images or start from scratch, and different modes of play.
- Various brush sizes and shapes – Includes triangles, lines, rectangles, dots, free style, stars, and more.
- Use images from you SD card – load any image saved on your Kindle Fire HD or Android device or choose from colorful clipart, then change any image you use or make into a fun puzzle game.

Overview:

This ad supported free app is great for any parent that wants to let their child go crazy with art. Children use their fingers to create brilliant works of art using different colors, shapes, and brush sizes. Start from scratch or upload an image from your memory card as your background and then choose from the huge variety of options and make your masterpiece!

Use one of the fun drawing effects like the kaleidoscope option which makes a 4-way mirror effect, and be as creative as you want. Quickly press undo to erase any mistakes. When you are done, there is an option to make a sliding puzzle out of your creation! This is sure to provide fun for your children to occupy them on long trips or anytime.

VeggieTales: The League of Incredible Vegetables

Price: $0.99 ($2.99 list price)
Purpose: A VeggieTales movie made into a game app for fun and learning.

Key Benefits:
- Straight from the movie – The app game follows LarryBoy and friends through the same adventure as in the movie and even includes cut scenes.
- Familiar scenes and characters – Includes the characters and environments in 3D straight from the movie so you feel like you are in the movie.
- Easy touchscreen controls – Tap-and-Drag controls let you move and interact on your journey.
- Replay value – Play over and over again as you take each character through each mission to earn extra Courage Coins to buy powers and upgrades.

Overview:
In VeggieTales: The League of Incredible Vegetables, LarryBoy and friends face the evil Dr. Flurry. They must face their own fears to defeat Dr. Furry and keep the city out of a frozen future. Your children will enjoy the touch controls as they play with their favorite VeggieTales characters.

Made for ages four and up, this app game allows children to take their favorite characters through a variety of missions to defeat Dr. Flurry. Play 28 fun and challenging levels. Unlock powers and upgrades as you battle to save Bumblyburg from the evil Dr.'s plan. Enjoy scenes from the movie and interacting with 3D environments.

Minecraft Pocket Edition

Price: $6.99

Purpose: Fun for kids and adults, Minecraft has become the legos of the future! Enjoy this building and creation app anytime, anywhere on your Kindle Fire HP

Key Benefits:
- Build anything – Craft and build anything you can imagine.
- Variety – You can build with different types of blocks and chose from randomized worlds.
- Play with friends – Invite friends to play via local wireless network and save multiplayer worlds to your Kindle Fire HD or other Android device.

Overview:
Minecraft is one of the most popular crafting games today! With Pocket Edition, you can build anything you can imagine on the go. Use block, much like legos, to create your world any way you want it.

Play by yourself or with friends via local network. You can even save those multiplayer worlds that you and your friends create together on your Kindle Fire HD or other Android device. Great fun for kids and adults – build, play, create!

Sight Words Sentence Builder

Price: $1.99
Purpose: This app will educate your child on Sight Words, the fundamental building blocks for reading.

Key Benefits:
- Made for Kindle – This has been optimized for Kindle Fire.
- Learn Dolch Sight Words – Dolch Sight Words have been the standard for schools across the nation for many years to teach children basic reading skills.
- Fun sights and sounds – Colorful graphics, fun visuals, visual and audio feedback to help your child learn.

Overview:
Schools require your children to study Sight Words. They are an essential part of reading. They are the building blocks of language for your children. Now your children have the ability to learn the Dolch Sight Words anywhere and anytime on your Kindle Fire HD or other Android device.

This awesome application allows your children to have fun and play simple games to learn grade level Sight Words. Your children will learn to put together short sentences in an entertaining way by receiving visual and auditory queues and feedback.

Productivity apps

In this section, we look at the top 5 most useful productivity apps. These apps help get you organized and keep you moving in the fast-paced business world. We've chosen the following 5 apps based on their usefulness and effectiveness and helping you be more productive, though they may be useful in other areas of life as well.

These apps are ideal for busy professionals who need help keeping track of important things like meetings and documents. They are useful to stay-at-home moms who school events like fundraisers and need to plan and stay on track. By utilizing these productivity applications no matter your situation, you will be better organized and experience increased productivity because of this.

Office Suite Professional 6

Price: $14.99
Purpose: Bring the office home! When your job requires more than the normal shift, you have access to all your documents right at your fingertips.

Key Benefits:
- Full office features on the go – Availability of every Office program (including Word, Excel, and PowerPoint) on your Kindle Fire HD or Android device.
- Print no matter where you are – Use Google Cloud Print or another compatible print software to print documents or PDFs over Wi-Fi.
- View charts and images – In the Excel module, you can use the embedding feature to see charts or images right in the spreadsheet or them yourself.

Overview:
This is a full-featured office right on your Kindle Fire HD or other Android device. OfficeSuite Professional 6 gives you the ability to integrate Google Docs. It is also compatible with many other programs such as Microsoft SkyDrive.

This program supports many versions of Microsoft Office from 97 up to 2010 and the newest version DOCX. With this app you have every ability that you have from your work or home PC using Microsoft Office programs. This app is sure to increase your productivity any time you're on the go.

iTranslate

Price: $0.00
Purpose: Translate what you need to when you need to.

Key Benefits:
-A wide variety of languages – this translator comes ready with over 50 languages.
– Dictionary – there are many dictionaries available right in the program to give you even more choices for your translation results.
– Voice recognition – iTranslate features voice recognition software so that you can speak and instantly see your translation.
– Optimized for tablet use – iTranslate this optimized and ready to be used on your Kindle Fire HD or other Android tablet.

Overview:
With languages from Arabic to French Latvian Swedish Ukrainian and even the enemies, iTranslate is a full-featured translation software they give you many options and many different features.

Some popular features include a variety of dictionaries, voice recognition, and the ability to share, save and copy. iTranslate is sure to increase your productivity any time you're dealing with documents requiring different languages.

Dropbox

Price:
$0.00

Purpose: Allows you to access your Dropbox account from your Kindle Fire HD or Android device.

Key Benefits:
– Access anywhere – With the Dropbox have you always have your files no matter where you are or what you're doing.
– Share your files easily – With just the click of a button you can share your photos and documents with friends and family.

Overview:
Dropbox is free to use and keeps all your files in one place that is used to access. No matter where you are, we can easily look at your photos, documents, videos and other files that you have saved in Dropbox.

From your Kindle Fire HD or other Android device you can add files to your Dropbox, and they will automatically be saved to all your computers. If you need to make changes to your documents, you can do it by accessing your files right in Dropbox. There is no need to wait until you get to a computer.

Speaktoit Assistant

Price: $0.00
Purpose: The Speaktoit Assistant is the device allows you to talk to your device to open apps and use Web services.

Key Benefits:
– Just talk – This amazing app allows you to use speech to interact with your device.
– Search with ease – By saying just a few words you can easily find the information and services they need.
– Easy to use – There are no complex interfaces and the no special commands they need to learn.
– Just like talking to a friend – Speak with terms they use in everyday conversation.

Overview:
The Speaktoit Assistant turns your Kindle Fire HD or Android device into your best friend by allowing you to use speech to do various things. You can do things like search for information, launch apps, and go to Google and Facebook.

There are no special commands or complex interfaces, so the app is very easy to use. All you need to do is talk to it just like you're talking to a friend. Use everyday language and conversation to do what you need to do.

ezPDF Reader

Price: $2.99
Purpose: To let you access and read PDFs from your Kindle Fire HD or other Android device.

Key Benefits:
– Easy access – ezPDF Reader gives you the ability to access your PDF documents no matter where you are.
– Voice reading – If you are busy or driving you can easily use the voice reading feature and have your documents read to you.
– Take notes – ezPDF Reader lets you take notes and make marks directly on the PDF documents.

Overview:
Accessing PDF documents on the go has never been this easy. Now you have the ability to open and read documents, make changes, and save your documents any time using your Kindle Fire HD or other Android device. Create folders to organize your PDF documents however you want them.

Get a thumbnail view of the pages making it easy to flip to the page that you need instead of going through the entire document. Driving or have your hands occupied? No problem! ezPDF Reader uses a voice feature to read your documents to you.

Lifestyles and Utilities Apps

In this section, we look at the top 5 lifestyles and utilities apps. These apps are helpful in everyday life for various reasons. They can help you get where you are going. They can help you out when you find yourself in a sticky situation. We've chosen the following 5 apps based on their ability to help you out when you need it the most or fit into your lifestyle to help keep you on track, though they will surely be useful in multiple areas of your daily life.

These apps are ideal for everyone! They provide you with basic tools to make life a little easier every day. By utilizing these lifestyles and utilities applications, you can take control of the uncertain times in your day.

Virtual Makeover

Price: $0.00

Purpose: Use your own photo or model pictures to try out new hairstyles and makeup ideas to see how they look before doing them on yourself.

Key Benefits:
– Create unlimited makeovers – Use your photo or one of the model photos to try out as many different looks as you can imagine.
– Hundreds of options – There are many different hairstyles and hair color combinations that you can create.
– Customize makeup – Choose from eye makeup lip color and accessories to make the perfect look.
– Share with your friends – With just one click you can share your makeover on Facebook, Twitter, and through e-mail right from your Kindle Fire HD.

Overview:
The Virtual Makeover app from Mary Kay allows you to try out various books with different hairstyles, color, and makeup without actually having to change your look in reality. You can select your own photo to see how the different styles would look on you.

You can even share your glamorous makeover by putting your face on the cover of "The Look" and sending it to your friends through Facebook or Twitter. Special features such as season specific makeovers, on-trend looks, and makeovers for special occasions are available with just a click.

Prayers & Blessings Daily

Price: $0.00
Purpose: To provide you with daily verses for inspiration.

Key Benefits:
– Choice of two version – You can switch between the English Standard Version and the classic King James Version.
– See the full verse with just one click – Each day a new verse will pop up and can be expanded by clicking on it to see the full verse.
– Inspire your friends – you can easily share the daily verse with your friends through social media or e-mail.

Overview:
Great for any Christian who is looking for new source of inspiration, the prayers and blessings daily app is just what you need. The on-screen widget will show you a new verse each day from either the English Standard Version or King James Version.

This makes a great addition to any other daily quote project that you have. The quotes can easily be shared with your friends by e-mail or by using the clipboard option to paste the Facebook or Twitter.

textPlus Free

Price: $0.00
Purpose: this app allows you to stay in touch with friends and family for free through texting.

Key Benefits:
– Unlimited free texting – The textPlus free version is an ad-supported app in which you get a phone number and can use it to send and receive unlimited free text.
– Extra free features – In addition to sending or receiving text, you can also group text and send and receive pictures for free.
– No phone needed – this app is available on your Kindle Fire HD and every Android device your own so there's no need to have a mobile phone.

Overview:
Do you frustrated with the charges from your mobile phone company? Now there's an alternative. GOGII provides this service for free because they believe it's important to stay connected with friends and family.

The free version of the app is ad-supported. There is also paid version available. Features include sending and receiving text, group text, extra messaging, and instant notification. The contents to anyone in the world that has this app.

7notes Premium – Smart Writing Tool

Price: $0.99
Purpose: Makes it easy to take notes anywhere, anytime.

Key Benefits:
– Take notes quickly and easily – You can quickly and easily take notes on your Kindle Fire HD.
– Handwriting recognition – 7notes includes a state-of-the-art in writing recognition engine to make it easier than ever to write your notes.
– Share your notes – You can export your notes to e-mail, Facebook, twitter, and more with just the click of a button.

Overview:
7notes Premium is a smart writing tool optimized for Kindle Fire. The app includes a unique handwriting recognition engine which makes it easier and better than ever to take notes.

Some of the features of the staff include the ability to take notes anytime anywhere, the ability to edit and decorate your notes, and an auto scroll feed feature which moves as you write. You can also export your notes to e-mail, Facebook, Evernote, Twitter and more.

SAS Survival Guide

Price: $0.99
Purpose: An easy-to-use guide for surviving a huge selection of situations.

Key Benefits:
– Survive any situation – The features in the sample teacher to survive nearly any situation no matter where you are.
– Easy-to-watch videos – The app includes 16 videos with survival tips that are easy to follow.
– Test your skills – by using the included survival checklist s and a quiz with over 100 questions, test your skills they've learned to see if you have what it takes to survive.

Overview:
The SAS Survival Guide is a unique that allows you to have the ability to survive and take it anywhere with you. This guide is newly available for Kindle beds are even sold millions times as a best-selling book and an iPhone/iPad app.

Written by John Wiseman, a former soldier, the app includes text videos and photos to teach you everything you need notice arrived nearly any situation. The photos included are of edible, medicinal and poisonous plants so that you can tell the difference. There's even a Morse code signaling device included. The search tool which you scan the entire book to find exactly what you need quickly.

Health and Fitness Apps

In this section, we look at the top 5 most useful health and fitness apps. These apps are designed with your benefit in mind. They will help you stay on track with your workout and weight loss goals. They can help you track your diet and provide you motivation to stay on track. We've chosen the following 5 apps based on their ability to improve your chances of reaching your health and fitness goals.

These apps are ideal for anyone concerned with their health and fitness. They will help you stay on track and focus without causing you extra stress. By utilizing these apps, you will be able to track your daily habits to make sure you are working toward your total health and fitness goals.

Rain Therapy: Rest, Relax, Unwind

Price: $0.99
Purpose: Relax and enjoy the sound of rain as it falls and clouds drift by your screen.

Key Benefits:
– Watch as you listen – Rain will fall and splatter on your screen as clouds slowly trip by while you listen to the four different rain sounds.
– Set the timer – choose from 15 min., 30 min., one hour, two hours, three hours, or nonstop rain.
– Many control options – You can pause and play the rain, control the intensity of the rain, control the size of the raindrops, and control the speed and direction that the sky moves.

Overview:
Rain Therapy is an app that gives you rain anytime you want it. In addition to displaying the current time and date, the interface is very easy to use and has a minimalist style. Choose from four different rain sounds and watches the rain splatters on your screen and clouds drift by.

Using your Kindle Fire HD, you can listen to the rain anytime whether you are going to bed, working, or reading. The relaxing and calming sound of rain is at your fingertips whenever you want.

Calorie Counter and Diet Tracker by MyFitnessPal

Price: $0.00

Purpose: Allows you to stay on track with you dieting goals by entering foods, exercises, and even entire meals.

Key Benefits:

– Very popular and widely used – featured in USA Today and on NBC and CNET; has nearly 1700 five-star ratings on Amazon.

– Comprehensive database – contains over 1,700,000 foods and gaining more each day.

– Many entry options – you can scan barcodes, or type in your foods in the search bar, adding exercises and even put an entire meals one time.

Overview:

The Calorie Counter has become a very popular way to keep track of your food and exercise and stay on track with your diet. You can easily search for foods in the comprehensive database or scan barcodes to enter the foods that you have eaten.

Create an account and sign up with MyFitnessPal and you're ready to go. Set up realistic goals for yourself and track your calorie intake and your exercise to see how much you lost over the time. You can choose from options that best fit your lifestyle such as sedentary if you sit often during the day or active if you're up and going a lot. With this app you be entering into a very supportive community that includes thousands of people just like you looking to keep track of their dieting and exercise.

All-in Yoga (Kindle Tablet Edition)

Price: $1.99

Purpose: All-in Yoga is a comprehensive learning tool including many pictures and guides to help you move through your choice of program.

Key Benefits:

– HD quality –Poses and photo, videos and audio guides with excellent graphic quality.

– Choose the best program for you – Over 40 yoga programs ready to go or you can create your own.

– A variety of poses and models – over 300 poses in vivid photos as well as 3-D muscle models for every pose.

– Get the help you need – Live support right in the app available for free.

Overview:

All-in Yoga is a comprehensive yoga program available on your Kindle Fire HD. It includes over 300 poses with HD quality photos, videos, and audio guides. There are even 3-D muscle models for every pose to show you which muscle groups you are working with each move.

The app also includes over 30 breathing exercises. Each exercise includes detailed instructions. There are over 40 yoga programs ready to go and you have the ability to create your own. Live support is available right in the app for free so you always have help when you need it.

WebMD (Kindle Tablet Edition)

Price: $0.00

Purpose: Access to all the information that is available on WebMD from anywhere at any time.

Key Benefits:

– Symptom Checker – Simply select the part of the body that's bothering you, choose your symptoms, and find out what conditions are issues could possibly be affecting you.

– Conditions – Find the information that is relevant to you and your condition and learn more about the related symptoms.

– Treatments – get extensive information on available drugs, supplements, and other treatments.

– Pill identification –use the handy Pill Identification Tool to make sure that you have the right medication in your bottles and to identify any medicine that you find lying around.

Overview:

WebMD is a great place to find all the information you need on various medications. Now you have the power right in your hands on your Kindle Fire HD. Choose from many options including Symptom Checker, Drugs and Treatment, First Aid Essentials, or the Pill Identification Tool to find out what you need to know.

By signing and you can personalize your app and save drugs, conditions, and articles that are important to you. If you think something is wrong, answers you need are just a touch away.

Home Remedies (Free)

Price: $0.00
Purpose: To make home remedies available anytime you need them on your Kindle Fire HD.

Key Benefits:
- Includes all information from the book – The Complete Guide to Home Remedies and Natural Cures for Common Ailments has been turned into an easy-to-use app.
- Cure problems naturally – Use this as a guide to find natural remedies to common problems that are safer than medications from doctors.
- Search by symptom – using the quick symptom search you can easily find exactly what you are looking for.

Overview:
The Complete Guide to Home Remedies has been a long used book for curing ailments naturally. These remedies are trusted and passed down through the ages from our ancestors.

Save money and time by using the quick search option to find natural cures and avoid expensive drug store medications. The app contains natural remedies for hundreds of ailments including Acne, Hair loss, and even Ear Aches.

Sports Apps

In this section, we will look at the 5 most useful sports apps. These apps will be helpful mostly for sports fanatics, although anyone with an interest in sports will be able to make use of their unique features. We've chosen the following 5 apps based on how beneficial they are in all aspects of sports, including keeping up with your team and their stats, finding out when games are being played, and keeping up with the latest stats.

These apps are ideal for any sports fan who would like to have a better way to keep track of the things that are important to you. By utilizing these sports applications you'll find it easier to keep track of your team and have fun doing so.

NBA Game Time (Kindle tablet edition)

Price: $0.00

Purpose: Use this official NBA tablet app to follow your favorite sports team and all of the NBA.

Key Benefits:
– Live stats – Get updated team and player stats as they happen.
– Video recaps – See video recaps of full games.
– Standings – Get league statistics and schedules and keep up-to-date on standings for the whole NBA.

Overview:
NBA Game Time is the official tablet app for the NBA. Stay up-to-date by following your team and all the teams of the NBA. Watch video recaps of full games right from your Kindle Fire HD.

Check-in often to see live updates the stats for your favorite teams and players. With just a few swipes of the finger you can get league statistics and schedule information. Which are NBA league Pass you can access live regular-season games by clicking setting and then entering your NBA league Pass Broadband Screen Name and password.

ESPN ScoreCenter

Price: $0.00

Purpose: ESPN ScoreCenter allows you to get all the latest scores, stats, and news on your Kindle Fire HD.

Key Benefits:

– Latest highlights – Keep up-to-date with the latest scores, stats, and the news any time no matter where you are.

– Easy interface – You can navigate easily to find what you're looking for with the smooth interface.

– Everything you want to see on one screen – You'll find all the details about your favorite teams on one screen making everything easy to keep up with.

Overview:

Each sport has their individual apps, however with ESPN Sports Center you'll find all your favorite teams in one place. This set includes everything you want to know about every sport around the world.

You can personalize your scoreboards to get live game details and up-to-the-minute scores and highlights. With my teams you can follow your favorite teams on one card. Watch videos and news reports right from your Kindle Fire HD. This is the must-have app for any sports fan.

Yahoo! Fantasy Football '12

Price: $0.00
Purpose: Manage your fantasy team and see stats in real-time.

Key Benefits:
- Live scoring – Real time updates of your team, league, and players stats during the game.
- Manage your team – View and change your lineup easily.
- Message boards – Get full access to message boards once your league drafts.

Overview:
Fantasy football players everywhere must have this app! Yahoo! Fantasy Football '12 is the newest in the series. You will have the access you need to make changes to your lineup right when you need to. Player get injured? No problem, get a new player right away from your Kindle Fire HD or Android device.

Get up to the minute stats and news as it happens during games. You will have access to everything you need to bring your league to the top. Stay on top of who is hot and who's not, injuries, bye weeks and make adjustments as you get the news. You can stay ahead of the game by having access during the game!

College Football Scoreboard

Price: $0.00
Purpose: An app dedicated to giving you the latest updates in college football.

Key Benefits:
– Get up-to-the-minute information – You can view the latest scores, schedules, and news for your favorite college teams.
– Historical game data – In addition to the latest updates, you can get historical information on any college game.

Overview:
College Football Scoreboard was created by Smartphones Technologies to give you the latest in college football information. Get up-to-the-minute scores, schedules, and player information for any of your favorite teams.

Conferences included are the ACC, Big 12, Big East, Big Ten, Pac-10 and many more. Learn about the history of the game, in addition to the bowl game stats and past wins. Be in the know with news when it happens.

MLB.com At Bat Lite

Price: $0.00

Purpose: This app gives you access to breaking news, schedules, and other updates for your favorite MLB teams.

Key Benefits:

– Customize your home screen – feature your favorite team on At Bat's home screen even the customizable options.
– Install the widget – With the MLB icon home screen widgets you can see and progress scores from around the league.
– Get breaking news – See the latest scores and highlights from every game right from your Kindle Fire HD.

Overview:

MLB.com At Bat Lite provide you with interactive rosters, player stats, breaking news and schedules for every team. Customize your home screen and install the MLB icon which it to get in game progress and up-to-the-minute scores around the league.

This is the official Major League Baseball app optimized for Kindle fire HD. For additional features, purchase the full version and get access to radio broadcast and video archives.

Entertainment Apps

In this section, we will look at the 5 most useful entertainment apps. These apps will be helpful when you're looking for some fun or just want to watch some entertaining videos and have a few laughs. We've chosen the following 5 apps based on their popularity, their entertainment factor, and their overall fun rating.

These apps are ideal for everyone who wants to have a laugh. If you're looking for some fun on your Kindle fire HD, utilize these entertainment applications and you're guaranteed to have a great time. Whether you're looking for movies, illusions, or some fun with an old scanner radio these are the apps for you.

Netflix

Price: $0.00 (Membership required)
Purpose: Use your account to access your favorite shows and movies anytime on your Kindle Fire HD or other Android device.

Key Benefits:
- Watch anytime – Just pull out your Kindle Fire HD and you are ready to watch your favorite shows and movies anytime.
- Resume feature – If you get interrupted while watching, you can use resume to start right where you left off.
- Quick search – Search by title or genre to find exactly what you want quickly.

Overview:
Use your Netflix account on your Kindle Fire HD anytime you want to watch a show or movie. Instant access, instant queue, and all the available Netflix features make it feel like you are watching on your TV or PC.

Save your favorites to watch over and over, set up a queue to move from one movie or show to the next without interruption, and just click Resume if you get interrupted and want to go back where you left off. Optimized for Kindle Fire, Netflix gives you hours of access to the streaming content that you want to watch.

Hulu Plus (Kindle Tablet Edition)

Price: $0.00 (Requires subscription; risk-free 1-week trial then $7.99/month with limited ads)
Purpose: Stream hit TV shows and movies to your Kindle Fire HD anytime.

Key Benefits:
- Full seasons of shows – Current season episodes and full previous seasons available to stream.
- Hit shows – Popular TV shows and hit movies like The Daily Show with Jon Stewart, Battlestar Galactica, The Office, Grey's Anatomy and more.

Overview:
Enjoy your favorite hit television shows and movies streaming straight to your Kindle Fire HD. 1-week risk free trial is available on the Hulu website. Subscriptions start at $7.99 per month with limited ads.

Gain access to hundreds of movies from all genres. Watch the current season episodes of popular television shows as well as full previous seasons. Get unlimited streaming to your Kindle and enjoy your favorites anytime.

Ghost Radar: LEGACY

Price: $0.99

Purpose: Have fun playing with the unknown as you tap into paranormal activity everywhere you go.

Key Benefits:
- Get real measurements – Measure electromagnetic energy and sounds even if you don't hear them.
- Record your sessions – Record and log your sessions of measurements and words that are picked up by the scanner.
- Two interfaces – Switch between a numerical interface and a graphical interface.

Overview:
Ghost Radar is an entertaining app that puts you in touch with your inner ghost hunter. Detect electromagnetic fields (considered to be the energy of spirits.) Record phantom words that are picked up through the sensitive scanner.

Adjust the sensitivity level to account for background noise and get a clearer audio sample. Display your information in numerical or graphical representations to easily see your results. This is for entertainment purposes only due to the lack of capability for scientific verification.

Eye Illusions Free 2.3

Price: $0.00

Purpose: Be amazed at the tricks your eyes can play on you with this wonderful collection of optical illusions.

Key Benefits:

- Lots of illusions – Enjoy hours of fun fooling your eyes with 3D illusions, weird lines, hidden objects and more.
- Easy navigation – Move quickly from one gallery to the next and one image to the next with a swipe of the finger.

Overview:

Enjoy tricking your eyes with this amazing illusion app. You will see appearing objects, color illusions, motion illusions and more as you navigate the galleries.

Use slideshow mode to go from one image to the next in a set time interval or switch manually when you are ready. Images come to life and fool you giving your eyes and your brain great pleasure.

Scanner Radio Pro

Price: $2.99
Purpose: Find the top scanners with the most listeners in your area.

Key Benefits:
- Updated lists – The list of the top 50 scanners near you updates every 5 minutes.
- Favorites list – Make a list of your favorite scanners to access them quickly.
- Directory – Browse the directory of scanners by genre or location including public safety, air traffic, weather and more.

Overview:
Ever wanted to listen in to local police scanners without purchasing expensive equipment? Now you can with Scanner Radio Pro. Listen in on the top scanners in your local area anytime on your Kindle Fire HD.

Over 2,900 scanners are available to choose from with more added daily including police and fire, amateur radio, and weather radios. Get notification alerts when a lot of people join a scanner to let you know something may be going on. Get you area added if it is not available by following on-screen instructions in the app menu.

Game Apps

In this section we will look at the top 5 most useful game apps. These apps are purely to play for fun. We've chosen the following 5 apps based on the fact that they are popular and considered to be very fun.

These apps are ideal for those of you looking to take a break from your busy lives and have a good time. By utilizing these game applications you are sure to have a smile on your face and relax a little bit while playing them.

Cut the Rope

Price: $0.99

Purpose: Feed little Om Nom the candy in a variety of different ways.

Key Benefits:
- Loads of levels – 300 levels in a variety of box types.
- Cute graphics – Unique and cute character and fun animations.
- Interesting gameplay – New gameplay physics and many free updates with new content to keep you playing.

Overview:
Om Nom is a cute little monster uniquely designed for this app where you "cut the rope" to feed him candy. Satisfy your little monster's sweet tooth and collect gold stars to unlock new levels.

Box types include Cardboard, Fabric, Gift Box, Toy Box and more. Each level is different with different mechanics to keep the game fun and interesting. There are 12 boxes that include 300 levels.

Andoku Sudoku 2 Free

Price: $0.00

Purpose: Solve unique number puzzles anytime you want to take a break from your daily routine.

Key Benefits:

- Tons of variety – Six Sudoku varieties with eight difficulty levels and 10,000 total puzzles.
- Mistakes are no problem – Fix your errors with unlimited times to redo or undo your moves.
- Interactive with a paper feel – Your finger gives pencil marks just like you would leave on paper.

Overview:

Created for beginners and pros, Andoku Sudoku 2 Free edition offers hours of gameplay fun. There are many combinations of levels and Sudoku varieties to create 10,000 unique puzzles.

If you make a mistake you can simply undo or redo to correct it and continue until you solve the puzzle. There is no limit to corrections. Optimized for phones and tablets, use your Kindle Fire HD to enjoy such Sudoku varieties as Standard, X-Sudoku, Hyper Sudoku and more anytime.

Angry Birds Space HD (Kindle Tablet Edition)

Price: $2.99 (On sale now $1.49)
Purpose: Navigate gravitational fields to slingshot the Angry Birds crew through space.

Key Benefits:
- Lots of gameplay – 140 Levels for hours of fun!
- New content – Enjoy new birds and new superpowers and even hidden bonus levels.
- Stellar graphics – This interstellar adventure features amazing graphics optimized for Kindle Fire HD with extremely detailed backgrounds and characters.

Overview:
Play this dynamic physics-based game where gravitational pull affects the movement of your Birds you utilize their new superpowers to move through puzzles and destroy environments to win! Journey through planets, black holes, stars and more as you seek to defeat the evil pigs and bring peace back to the galaxy.

Free updates keep the game content fresh with new levels, birds and superpowers. Unlock bonus content like levels inspired by classic games. Relax and play whenever you have a few minutes free with your Kindle Fire HD.

Asphalt 7: Heat (Kindle Tablet Edition)

Price: $0.99
Purpose: Gives racing and driving simulation fans access to an amazing collection of vehicles and tracks to race to victory.

Key Benefits:
- Variety of great cars – 60 popular cars from well-known manufacturers.
- Great scenery – 15 tracks in real cities like Hawaii, Paris, and Miami.
- Social racing – Compare race stats, challenge your pals, and share achievements through social media.

Overview:
This latest addition to the famous Asphalt racing series, Asphalt 7: Heat gives players an opportunity to race 60 awesome cars on 15 beautiful tracks set in popular cities around the world. Choose from one of six game modes with 150 different races.

Graphics are genius as the tracks take you through popular cities around the world and give you a never-before-seen view. Share your stats with your friends and even challenge them to some friendly racing competition with the new social media features.

Pac-Man

Price: $2.99

Purpose: Pac-Man is a quick paced game in which you use hand-eye coordination to collect pellets and run away from ghost.

Key Benefits:

– Classic version – This version of Pac-Man optimized for Kindle Fire is just like the original arcade game.

– Familiar gameplay – This version is played exactly like the original game and even included the original music and sound effects, but now you can play it anytime anywhere and swipe your finger to change directions.

– Old characters, new fun – take Pac-Man through each maze eating pellets on his way to victory while avoiding the familiar ghost Blinky, Pinky, Inky, and Clyde.

Overview:

This classic game is sure to bring back memories for adults and be a lot of fun for kids. In Pac-Man, you use quick movement to eat pellets and keep the ghost from eating you.

On your Kindle Fire HD, you move by flicking the screen to change direction. You can also use the PAC-PAD which simulates the joystick and slide your finger to move. Enjoy the familiar sounds and music from the arcade game and you chomp your way from one level to the next.

News & Magazines Apps

In this section, we will look at the top 5 most useful News & Magazine apps. These apps are the best ones to depend on for news and information. We've chosen the following 5 apps because they are the best in their category for providing information, unbiased news reports and entertainment news.

These apps are ideal for those of you that want to stay up-to-date on the most pressing issues. If you are looking for a great way to stay informed on the go, utilizing these News and Magazine applications you will do just that.

Wall Street Journal (Fire App/WSJ Digital)

Price: $0.00 (Requires subscription for full access $21.62 per month)

Purpose: To provide you with the Wall Street Journal's award-winning coverage any time on the Kindle Fire HD.

Key Benefits:

– Risk-free trial – Enjoy a 30 day risk-free trial to decide if you want to commit to the monthly fee for full access.

– Experience the best content – The Wall Street Journal provides award-winning coverage with sections including Opinion, Marketplace, Personal Journal, and other free articles.

Overview:

The Wall Street Journal has provided award-winning coverage for many years. There is a lot of free access to game by downloading the app including sections such as What's New, Money and Investing, Greater New York, and the WSJ Weekend Edition.

Start your subscription and enjoy the many special features including the full Wall Street Journal published every morning, the "Now Edition" updated throughout the day, and the availability to save articles to read later. By subscribing for just $21.62 per month, you also gain access to the 7-day archive downloadable for reading any time even when you're off-line.

NBC Nightly News

Price: $0.00
Purpose: To provide you with everything you expect from the NBC nightly news on your Kindle Fire HD or other Android device.

Key Benefits:
– Browse the latest headlines – With a few strokes of the finger you can scroll through the latest news story headlines and details from the nightly news.
– Watch full broadcast – If you missed the most recent broadcast you can watch the entire video on your Kindle Fire HD
– Share with your friends – You can easily share your favorite stories with your friends via Facebook, twitter, or e-mail.

Overview:
From the cutting edge news that you have grown to trust to health and science reports and making a difference profiles, everything you're looking for is available for free on the NBC Nightly News App. Read the blog of Brian Williams, watch the latest news report, and get today's headlines with a few taps of the finger.

You can set up auto-play to watch videos in sequence and read all the top stories and headlines on ABC news.com. Get news you trust from around the globe, political coverage, and all the best headlines for free anytime no matter where you are.

TIME Magazine

Price: $0.00 (Requires subscription; 1-month $2.00, 1-year $29.99, non-subscription single issue $4.99)

Purpose: Access your TIME Magazine subscription enhanced for Kindle Fire HD and get the latest from one of the world's most trusted news sources.

Key Benefits:
- Instant access – Enjoy your print subscription anytime from your Kindle Fire HD
- News you will want to read – TIME magazine is known for great content told in a matching tone.
- Extra content – Kindle users gain access to special content in addition to the regular issues.

Overview:
TIME magazine has been long known for its trusted content. Publishing some of the best stories, TIME grabs it readers and challenges them to think as the keep up with the latest stories.

Optimized for Kindle Fire HD, TIME magazine offers its tablet readers bonus content and extra photos and videos. Get live updates from Time.com and access to the complete TIME archive, including commemorative issues.

National Geographic Magazine

Price: $0.00 (Requires subscription; Annual subscription $19.99, Single issue $4.99)

Purpose: Enjoy the fantastic photography and ground reporting from the magazine conveniently anytime on your Kindle Fire HD.

Key Benefits:

- Free with download – Enjoy an exclusive edition of "Exploring Space: Journeys to the Edge of the Universe" just for downloading the app.
- Beautiful photography – Check out the wondrous photography straight from the magazine no matter where you are without carrying it around with you as it is optimized for Kindle Fire.
- Automatic subscription renewal – Keep up-to-date with one of the world's most fascinating magazines and never miss an issue with the option of automatic subscription renewal of 12 issues for just $19.99 per year.

Overview:

On-the-ground reporting and amazing photography have always been expected from National Geographic magazine. You can continue to expect this excellence and get it right on your Kindle fire HD with this brand-new app.

Optimized for Kindle fire, National Geographic magazine offers exclusive content and enhanced functionality. Enjoy the photo galleries, videos, and content you can trust and never miss an issue with automatic subscription renewal.

PEOPLE Magazine

Price: $0.00 (Requires subscription; 1-month $9.99, 6-month $54.99; Single issue without subscription $3.99)
Purpose: Use your Kindle Fire HD to access your PEOPLE Magazine subscription.

Key Benefits:
- Access your subscription anywhere – With a subscription you get free access to all issues of PEOPLE Magazine on your Kindle Fire HD.
- Lots of extras – You'll have exclusive access to extra Star Tracks pictures and bonus Celebrity photos.
- Stay up-to-date faster than ever – Exclusive access provides you breaking news and the top stories the moment they are available on your tablet.

Overview:
With the PEOPLE Magazine app you can get the app for free then buy single issues or purchase a subscription to get free access to every issue. Especially designed for Kindle Fire, you will get great content and swipe and tap your way through each page.

Enjoy bonuses like tablet-only photo galleries. You can see the latest TV reviews and movie trailers. Your subscription will automatically renew so that you never miss an issue!

www.ingramcontent.com/pod-product-compliance
Lightning Source LLC
LaVergne TN
LVHW052314060326
832902LV00021B/3877